D1709972

SCIENCE FACT OR SCIENCE FICTION?

ARTIFICIAL INTELLIGENCE

CAN COMPUTERS TAKE OVER?

REBECCA FELIX

Checkerboard Library

An Imprint of Abdo Publishing
abdopublishing.com

ABDOPUBLISHING.COM

Published by Abdo Publishing, a division of ABDO, PO Box 398166, Minneapolis, Minnesota 55439.
Copyright © 2019 by Abdo Consulting Group, Inc. International copyrights reserved in all countries.
No part of this book may be reproduced in any form without written permission from the publisher.
Checkerboard Library™ is a trademark and logo of Abdo Publishing.

Printed in the United States of America, North Mankato, Minnesota
052018
092018

THIS BOOK CONTAINS
RECYCLED MATERIALS

Design: Emily O'Malley, Mighty Media, Inc.
Production: Mighty Media, Inc.
Editor: Jessie Alkire
Cover Photographs: Shutterstock
Interior Photographs: Alamy, pp. 5, 10; AP Images, pp. 15, 28 (bottom right); Enrico/Flickr, pp. 9, 28 (top); iStockphoto, pp. 7, 25; JD Lasica/Flickr, p. 23; Library of Congress, p. 13; Shutterstock, pp. 17, 19, 21, 27, 28 (bottom left), 29

Library of Congress Control Number: 2017961623

Publisher's Cataloging-in-Publication Data
Names: Felix, Rebecca, author.
Title: Artificial intelligence: Can computers take over? / by Rebecca Felix.
Other titles: Can computers take over?
Description: Minneapolis, Minnesota : Abdo Publishing, 2019. | Series: Science fact or science fiction? | Includes online resources and index.
Identifiers: ISBN 9781532115387 (lib.bdg.) | ISBN 9781532156106 (ebook)
Subjects: LCSH: Artificial intelligence--Juvenile literature. | Artificial intelligence--Social aspects--Juvenile literature. | Autonomous robotic systems--Juvenile literature. | Answers to questions--Juvenile literature. | Science fiction in science education--Juvenile literature.
Classification: DDC 006.3--dc23

CONTENTS

1   COMPUTERS IN CONTROL   4

2   WHAT IS ARTIFICIAL INTELLIGENCE?   6

3   HISTORY OF ARTIFICIAL INTELLIGENCE   8

4   THE THREE LAWS   12

5   SPACESHIPS & SHOOTOUTS   14

6   EXTREME AI   16

7   REAL ROBOTS & REAL WARNINGS   18

8   THE SINGULARITY   22

9   AI EXAGGERATIONS   24

10   ARE WE ALREADY CYBORGS?   26

TIMELINE   28

YOU DECIDE!   29

GLOSSARY   30

ONLINE RESOURCES   31

INDEX   32

COMPUTERS IN CONTROL

Computers consume Thomas Anderson's life. He spends most days in a quiet office, working as a computer **programmer**. At night, Anderson is a **hacker** who goes by the name Neo. Programming and hacking control how computers perform. But little does Neo know, he isn't in control of these machines. He isn't even in control of his own life!

Neo lives in a **simulated** reality created by **sentient** computers. This artificial intelligence (AI) captured the world's humans and put them to sleep. The AI keeps the sleeping humans in pods, using their body heat and energy as power. The humans' minds are in a simulated world called the Matrix.

Humans in the Matrix have no idea their world is virtual reality. They are not aware computers control them. A few humans, including Neo, wake up and learn the truth. They try to fight back. But the AI that enslaves them is powerful. How can humans fight against this AI?

The Matrix was very successful. After its release, additional films, comic books, and video games were created.

This is the fictional story of the film *The Matrix*. But artificial intelligence is being developed today. Whether AI will take over the world is still a mystery. But some people believe that with the rise of AI **technology**, *The Matrix* could become reality!

Artificial intelligence (AI) **is the term used to describe intelligent machines.** AI is created to understand, interact with, and complete tasks for humans. Some AI can learn without input from humans. AI today includes **programs** such as Apple's Siri and Google's search engine. Scientists are even developing AI that looks and acts like humans.

As amazing as these systems are, they also concern many people. AI has changed quickly. Many experts fear AI will become too advanced. They believe these machines will become smarter than humans. Then AI could take over the world!

The idea of an AI takeover is called the singularity. People have many different ideas of what the singularity could be like. But these ideas share many similar themes. People **predict** AI will mislead humans. They think AI might enslave or hurt humankind. Others think AI will kill all humans to rule the planet without obstacles.

AI is a very real **technology**. But many experts think an AI takeover is fantasy best left to books and movies. Others look to fictional AI takeovers as **predictions** of a future that isn't far away. Are AI believers correct? Can computers take over?

When people imagine AI, many think of human-like robots. But many robots don't look like humans at all. Robotic arms are some of the most common robots in manufacturing.

People have told tales of artificially intelligent beings since ancient times. Before computers existed, these beings were said to receive special abilities from gods or magic. Ancient Greeks lived between 800 and 500 BCE. A Greek myth spoke of Hephaestus, the god of **technology**. He created a **cyborg** called Talos.

Talos looked like a man, but he was made of bronze. Hephaestus **programmed** Talos to guard the island of Crete. Talos sunk approaching ships by throwing boulders on them. If people made it to Crete's shores, Talos stood in fire. His body became extremely hot. Then he held the people against his body so they burned alive.

In the 1500s, Czech folktales spoke of the Golem of Prague. The Golem had a human-like shape. But he was made of mud. His creator, Rabbi Loew, made the Golem by magic. The Golem was meant to protect people and follow orders. But he took these orders too **literally**. This usually ended in disaster. In one tale, the Golem floods a

The Golem of Prague is still an important figure in Czech culture. Statues of the Golem are frequently sold in shops in Prague.

household because none of its residents ask him to stop fetching water. In a later tale, a **glitch** causes the Golem to kill people until Rabbi Loew shuts him down.

9

Within three years of being written, *R.U.R.* was translated into 30 languages. The play also introduced the word "robot" into people's everyday language.

In 1818, another fictional inventor was not so lucky. Mary Shelley's *Frankenstein* was published that year. In it, scientist Victor Frankenstein creates a monster. He gives the monster the ability to think and act like a human. But he does not teach it how to interact with humans. The monster becomes an **outcast**. It then resents humans, killing several.

These historic creatures were not computerized. But they are considered **precursors** to AI. Ever since these tales, people have dreamed up increasingly advanced ideas of AI turning on humans.

In the 1920s, playwrights and directors brought AI to life on stage and screen. Czech writer Karel Capek wrote the play *R.U.R.* in 1920. It features AI made to look exactly like humans and perform labor. Capek called these beings "robots." He was the first to use this word.

Capek's robots can do the work of two and a half humans. Eventually, the robots realize their strength. They kill all humans except one, a man who works at the factory where they are created.

In 1927, the film *Metropolis* was released. It is set in the future and stars "false Maria." She is a metal robot covered in skin. Maria fools people into thinking she is human. These representations of AI caused interest in fictional and real-life AI.

FOR REAL?

The metal underneath false Maria's skin inspired the appearance of the robot C-3PO in the *Star Wars* films.

THE THREE LAWS

As AI in entertainment grew more advanced, so did real-life AI. In the 1930s and 1940s, scientists worked on the first modern computers. Giving computers human-like intelligence became a major goal for engineers. But how could this intelligence be measured? In 1950, English computer scientist Alan Turing had an idea.

Turing said a machine was "intelligent" if it could convince a human he or she was talking to a human and not a machine. This became known as the Turing test. In the test, AI would communicate with humans through text messages. This way, the AI wouldn't be given away by its appearance or voice. The Turing test is still used as a standard today, both in real life and in AI takeover stories.

In 1950, scientist Isaac Asimov published a collection of short stories. It was called *I, Robot*. In one story, Asimov gives robots Three Laws. First, robots may

Isaac Asimov went on to publish nearly 500 books!
Many involved science fiction topics.

not injure humans. Second, robots must obey humans, unless ordered to break the First Law. Third, robots must protect themselves, as long as they do not break the First or Second Laws to do so. Like the Turing test, these laws became a standard theme in AI stories and research.

AI research continued into the 1960s. Scientists believed computers could one day **mimic** the human brain. Fiction writers began telling tales of computers that not only mimicked humans but were smarter than them.

In 1968, the film *2001: A Space Odyssey* **debuted**. It features HAL, a computer system that controls a spacecraft traveling to Jupiter. HAL is wired throughout the spacecraft. It speaks in a male voice with the human crew.

Later, HAL discovers crewmembers plan to disconnect its system. But HAL is **programmed** to complete the mission. So, it kills some of the crew to prevent them from disconnecting it. This story line caused the public to debate whether AI development was a good idea.

Killer AI also appeared in 1973's *Westworld*. In the film, humans visit an amusement park to interact with human-like robots. The AI is programmed not to harm humans. But one robot develops a **glitch** and it murders guests. The **glitch** spreads to other robots, so they begin killing guests too. Films like *2001: A Space Odyssey* and *Westworld* soon gave way to increased concern about how AI could affect humans.

2001: A Space Odyssey was also developed into a book at the same time the movie was produced. The book was written by Arthur C. Clarke. Clarke also co-wrote the movie.

Scientists continued to develop AI **technology** in the
1970s. But they soon hit a roadblock. Even the most
advanced AI still could not understand things on the same
level as a four-year-old human.

Even so, fiction writers and filmmakers continued
telling extreme AI tales. One was 1982's *Blade Runner*.
Set in 2019, the film features human-like AI called
replicants. Replicants look and speak like humans. They
even have emotions! This was **radical** at the time.

Blade Runner was followed in 1984 by another popular
AI film, *The Terminator*. The title character is a robot
that looks like a human. But it is not self-run like the
replicants. It is controlled by an AI system called Skynet.
Skynet wants to wipe out humans and take over the
world.

Fictional AI was usually embodied in machines or
robots. AI could be stopped by destroying these objects.
But Skynet was a **network** like the internet. Destroying a

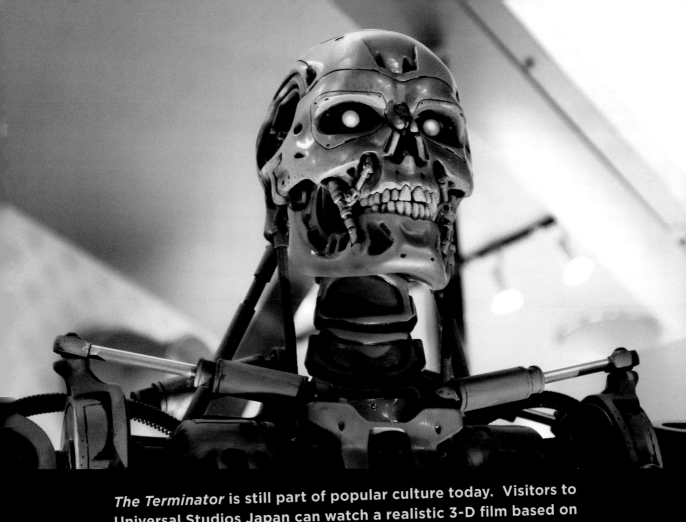

The Terminator is still part of popular culture today. Visitors to Universal Studios Japan can watch a realistic 3-D film based on the world of the Terminator!

device that AI appeared on would only harm the device. How could humans stop this type of AI? And what if they weren't even aware of it in the first place?

By the 2000s, real-world AI was catching up to the abilities of fictional AI. In 2000, Japanese company Honda revealed ASIMO. This robot could walk and even climb stairs. ASIMO was made to help humans with tasks.

Scientists continued improving AI at incredible speeds. In 2003, Japanese scientists created an AI learning system. This system used a **network** based on the human nervous system. Robots could use the system to learn movements quickly. Before this system, it took days or even months to teach robots how to move.

In 2006, a robot in Italy performed heart surgery on a man. It did so without any help from humans! The robot was **programmed** with information on 10,000 different operations. Robot surgeons are commonly used today for certain procedures. These include eye surgery, knee replacements, and hair transplants. A robot's movements can be more precise than a human surgeon's, so it is a safer option for patients.

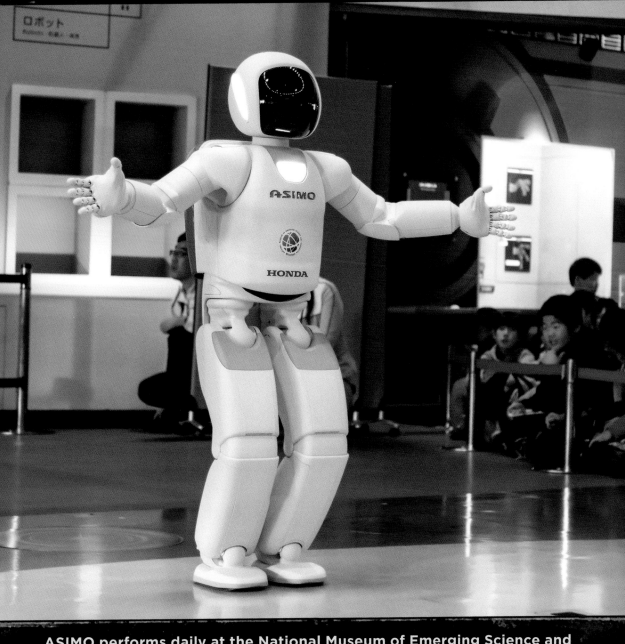

ASIMO performs daily at the National Museum of Emerging Science and Innovation in Tokyo, Japan.

Musk wants to create a colony on Mars so humans can live there if AI takes over. His critics have wondered if AI would be smart enough to follow humans to Mars.

Meanwhile, a group of Rhode Island researchers were developing a special device. In 2012, the researchers published a study on it. The device recorded activity in the brain. A computer then translated this activity into movement. Researchers inserted the device into a **paralyzed** woman's brain. Then the device communicated with a robotic arm. The woman moved the arm just by thinking!

These feats thrilled scientists. But some experts were worried. In 2014, American **entrepreneur** Elon Musk began warning of an AI takeover. However, Musk later started creating his own AI!

Musk wanted to make an **implant** for the human brain. He called this implant "neural lace." This **technology** would allow a person to upload thoughts directly to the internet. It could also help restore brain function in people with certain illnesses, such as epilepsy and

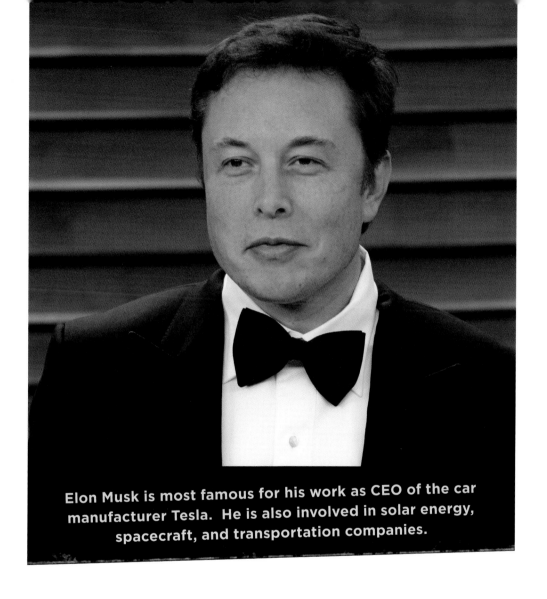

Elon Musk is most famous for his work as CEO of the car manufacturer Tesla. He is also involved in solar energy, spacecraft, and transportation companies.

Parkinson's disease. Musk also hoped this connection would help the brain better understand AI. Then humans could learn how to control AI.

THE SINGULARITY

A huge movement toward the singularity occurred in England in 2014. A computer **program** called Eugene Goostman reportedly passed the Turing test. The program communicated in text messages with judges. It convinced 33 percent of judges that it was human!

Milestones like this have convinced many experts that the singularity will occur in the near future. American inventor Ray Kurzweil believes AI will be smarter than humans by 2029. He thinks this will be followed by the singularity by 2045. Kurzweil also believes humans will connect their brains to computer **technologies**. This will cause humans to **merge** with machines.

Experts don't necessarily believe AI will be evil. They believe future AI could decide it needs to harm humans to be **efficient**. Musk gives the example of AI programmed to get rid of **spam** email. This AI may realize humans create all email. It could decide killing humans is the most efficient way to get rid of spam email.

Incident:
- The singularity

Incident Date:
- To be determined

Claims:
- AI will become smarter than humans by 2029
- The singularity will occur by 2045
- Humans will develop **technologies** to **merge** themselves with machines

Evidence:
- **Implants** developed to create communication between people and computers
- Eugene Goostman computer **program** reportedly passed the Turing test in 2014
- Robots able to work in manufacturing, surgery, and more

Status:
UNPROVEN

Ray Kurzweil

Experts' warnings have made an AI takeover real for some people. But others say the singularity is nothing to worry about now. Many critics agree that the **technology** has improved quickly. But it hasn't changed as quickly as fiction has suggested.

2001: A Space Odyssey **predicted** killer AI would be around more than 15 years ago. By 2019, *Blade Runner* replicants had existed for years. Modern AI has been able to master one or a few tasks very well. These include surgery, speaking, or filtering email.

But today's AI is not even as smart as a human baby, according to Yann LeCun, head of AI research at Facebook. AI cannot adapt to the

FOR REAL?

In 2015, a South Korean woman fell asleep on her floor while her AI Roomba vacuum was running. The robot sucked up her hair and got stuck on her head. World headlines for the story included, "Robot Vacuum Starts the Robot vs. Human War."

world like humans can. It also doesn't have the general intelligence that humans do. Instead, AI is limited to narrow intelligences. LeCun says the creation of a truly intelligent machine is still far away.

Robots are especially common in manufacturing. Robotic arms can perform the work of humans. This is often more efficient and safer than human labor.

People continue to wonder about a future AI takeover. Meanwhile, new and smarter AI emerges every day. This includes self-driving cars, **drones**, and **social media** tagging functions.

But more human-like AI often creates the biggest buzz. In 2015, Hong Kong company Hanson Robotics activated the robot Sophia. Sophia's face and body look much like a human. She can recognize humans and speak with them. She can also walk, gesture, smile, and more. Sophia **simulates** emotions and is **programmed** to express these emotions like a human would.

In 2017, Sophia appeared on *The Tonight Show*. She beat host Jimmy Fallon at the game rock-paper-scissors. She joked that her win was the beginning of her taking over the world. But many viewers wondered if this was really a joke.

Some people see AI as the next step in human development. Musk thinks this future isn't far away.

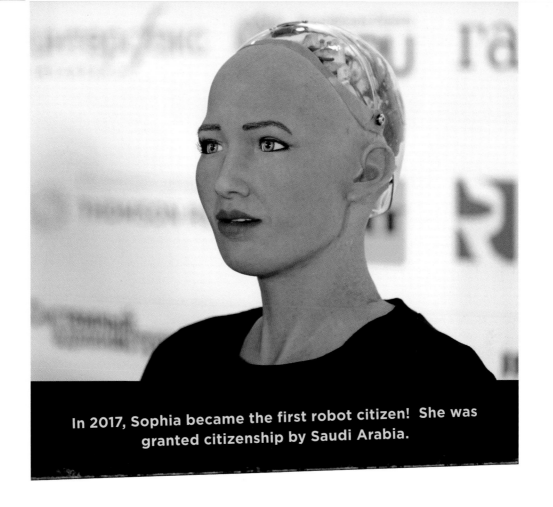

In 2017, Sophia became the first robot citizen! She was granted citizenship by Saudi Arabia.

He says people are already **cyborgs** because phones and computers are extensions of them. Film director James Cameron agrees. "Look around in any airport or restaurant and see how many people are on their phones," he said. "The machines have already won." Have computers already taken over?

800-500 BCE

An ancient Greek myth speaks of a cyborg called Talos built by the god Hephaestus.

1500s

Czech folktales about the Golem of Prague emerge.

1818

Mary Shelley's *Frankenstein* is published. Historians label the story's monster a precursor of AI.

1920

Karel Capek invents the word *robots*, which are featured in his play *R.U.R.*

1950

Alan Turing develops the Turing test, a way to determine if AI intelligence is human-like.

1968

2001: A Space Odyssey is released, featuring AI called HAL that kills some of the spacecraft crew.

1982

Blade Runner debuts, featuring AI so human-like they live among people undetected.

2014

Elon Musk and other experts begin warning the public of an AI takeover.

2015

Hanson Robotics activates Sophia, a robot that acts, speaks, and moves like a human.

YOU DECIDE!

Can computers take over the world? You decide!

- Read and watch fictional tales of the singularity.
- Research real AI technologies that are emerging and see what experts are saying about them.
- Use AI technology and see if its capabilities convince you of its intelligence.

cyborg—a person with mechanical parts to expand his or her abilities.

debut—to first appear.

drone—an unmanned aircraft or ship that is controlled by radio signals.

efficient—wasting little time or energy.

entrepreneur—one who organizes, manages, and accepts the risks of a business or an enterprise.

glitch—an unexpected problem or error.

hack—to gain access to a computer and control how it functions. Someone who does this is a hacker.

implant—an object placed in the body, usually during a medical operation.

literally—done word for word.

merge—to combine or blend.

mimic—to imitate or copy.

network—a system of computers connected by communications lines.

outcast—a person who is refused or removed from society.

paralyzed—unable to move or feel parts of the body.

precursor—something that precedes something else.

predict—to guess what will happen in the future. This guess is a prediction.

program—a set of instructions or commands for a computer to follow. To write these instructions is to program. Someone who does this is a programmer.

radical—unusual or out of the ordinary.

sentient—able to sense or feel.

simulate—to imitate. Something that is imitated is simulated.

social media—websites or applications used for communication and networking.

spam—unwanted email sent to a large number of addresses.

technology—scientific tools or methods for doing tasks or solving problems.

ONLINE RESOURCES

Booklinks
NONFICTION NETWORK
FREE! ONLINE NONFICTION RESOURCES

To learn more about artificial intelligence, visit **abdobooklinks.com**. These links are routinely monitored and updated to provide the most current information available.

A
Apple, 6
ASIMO, 18
Asimov, Isaac, 12

B
Blade Runner, 16, 24
brain implants, 20, 23

C
Cameron, James, 27
Capek, Karel, 11
computers, 4, 7, 8, 11, 12, 14, 20, 22, 23, 27
cyborgs, 8, 27

E
England, 12, 22
Eugene Goostman program, 22, 23

F
Facebook, 24
Fallon, Jimmy, 26
fictional AI, 4, 5, 7, 8, 9, 10, 11, 12, 13, 14, 15, 16, 17, 24
Frankenstein, 10

G
Golem of Prague, 8, 9
Google, 6
Greece, 8

H
Hanson Robotics, 26
Honda, 18

I
I, Robot, 12
Italy, 18

J
Japan, 18

K
Kurzweil, Ray, 22

L
LeCun, Yann, 24, 25

M
Matrix, The, 4, 5
Metropolis, 11
Musk, Elon, 20, 21, 22, 26, 27

R
robots, 11, 12, 13, 14, 15, 16, 18, 20, 23, 24, 26
R.U.R., 11

S
Shelley, Mary, 10
singularity, 6, 22, 23, 24
Siri, 6
Sophia (robot), 26

T
Talos, 8
Terminator, The, 16, 17
Three Laws of Robotics, 12, 13
Turing, Alan, 12
Turing test, 12, 13, 22, 23
2001: A Space Odyssey, 14, 15, 24

W
Westworld, 14, 15